PLANT CYCLE

NATURE'S CYCLES

Ray James

Rourke
Publishing LLC
Vero Beach, Florida 32964

www.rourkepublishing.com

PHOTO CREDITS: All Photographs © Lynn M. Stone, except p. 15 © Imee Beatrix Demeterio

Editor: Robert Stengard-Olliges

Cover and interior design by Nicola Stratford

Library of Congress Cataloging-in-Publication Data

James, Ray.
  Plant cycle / Ray James.
    p. cm. -- (Nature's cycle)
  ISBN 1-60044-180-7 (hardcover)
  ISBN 1-59515-537-6 (softcover)
  1. Plant life cycles--Juvenile literature. I. Title. II. Series: James, Ray. Nature's cycle.

QK49.S815 2007
580--dc22   2006014429

Printed in the USA

CG/CG

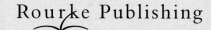

Rourke Publishing

www.rourkepublishing.com – sales@rourkepublishing.com
Post Office Box 3328, Vero Beach, FL 32964

Table of Contents

Plant Life Cycles

A plant's life cycle is the story of how it lives. There are thousands of different kinds of plants.

Some plants are quite small. Some are huge! The largest are the mighty redwood and sequoia trees of California.

Plant Reproduction

All plants make more plants of their own kind. This process is called **reproduction**. Without it, plants would disappear.

Plants have male and female parts. Those parts are often found in the center of a flower blossom.

Male parts make **pollen**. Pollen looks like brightly colored dust. The female parts make eggs called **ovules**.

Flowers attract insects and other animals. These animals help to brush pollen onto ovules.

Pollen and ovules together make seeds. Seeds are the keys to new plants.

Plant Seeds

Some **ripe** seeds drop from the plant. Other plant seeds move a great distance.

Wind blows some seeds from place to place. Birds carry some seeds away too.

Coconuts are seeds, too. Coconuts float. Oceans carry them from place to place.

Plant Growth

Seeds wait for the right time to **sprout**.

Desert wildflowers bloom only after ideal rainfall.

New growth springing from a seed is called **germination**. The new plant grows by using sunlight to make food.

Its leaves collect sunlight. Its roots gather water and vitamins from soil.

Plant lives may be short or long. The plant parts are not wasted when they die.

They break down into tiny bits of matter. They become part of the soil and water. They also become vitamins for new plants and animals!

Glossary

germination (JUR muh na shuhn) — when seeds begin to grow

ovules (AHW uules) — small eggs

pollen (POL uhn) — tiny yellow particles made by plants for reproduction

reproduction (ree pruh DUHK shuhn) — the making of more of the same plant or animal

ripe (RIPE) — seeds, fruit or vegitables that have finished growing

sprout (SPROUT) — to grow

INDEX

FURTHER READING

Kalman, Bobbie. *Life Cycle of a Flower*. Crabtree, 2004.
Fowler, Alan. *From Seed to Plant*. Scholastic, 2001.

WEBSITES TO VISIT

http://www.urbanext.uiuc.edu/gpe/case1/c1facts1b.html
http://www.arboretum.fullerton.edu/grow/primer/cycle.asp

ABOUT THE AUTHOR

Ray James writes children's fiction and nonfiction. A former teacher, Ray understands what kids like to read. Ray lives with his wife and three cats in Gary, Indiana.